BYRON KATIE

∾ on ∾

Love, Sex, and Relationships

Edited by Stephen Mitchell

BYRON KATIE INTERNATIONAL, INC. • LOS ANGELES

Copyright © 2006 by Byron Kathleen Mitchell.
All rights reserved. No part of this book may be reproduced in any form or by any means, electronic or mechanical, including photocopying, recording, or by any information storage and retrieval system, without permission in writing from the publisher, except by a reviewer, who may quote brief passages in a review.

Published in the United States by:
Byron Katie International, Inc.
578 Washington Blvd. Box 821
Marina del Rey, CA 90292
1-800-98KATIE (52843)
www.thework.com

ISBN 1-890246-78-6

Printed in the United States of America.
Design & Layout by Balsam Design
Art Director: Richard Balsam
Production Specialist: Emily Eoff
Cover Photography: Brie Childers

To Prem Rikta,
with gratitude for all the time she
put into compiling Katie's words

The Work of Byron Katie: The Four Questions and Turnaround

1. Is it true?
2. Can you absolutely know that it's true?
3. How do you react when you believe that thought?
4. Who would you be without the thought?

and

Turn it around.

Nothing outside you can ever give you what you're looking for.

Once we begin to question our thoughts, our partners, alive, dead, or divorced, are always our greatest teachers. There's no mistake about the person you're with; he or she is the perfect teacher for you, whether or not the relationship works out, and once you enter inquiry, you come to see that clearly. There's never a mistake in the universe. So if your partner is angry, good. If there are things about him that you consider flaws, good, because these flaws are your own, you're projecting them, and you can write them down, inquire, and set yourself free. People go to India to find a guru, but you don't have to. You're living with one. Your partner will give you everything you need for your own freedom.

When you don't love the other person, it hurts, because love is your very self. And you can't *make* yourself do it! You can't make yourself love someone. But when you come to love yourself, you automatically love the other person. You can't not. Just as you can't make yourself love us, you can't make yourself not love us. It's all your projection.

Personalities don't love; they want something. Love doesn't seek anything. It's already complete. It doesn't want, doesn't need, has no *shoulds* (not even for the person's own good). So when I hear people say that they love someone and want to be loved in return, I know they're not talking about love. They're talking about something else.

I can't feel angry at my partner without suffering. This doesn't feel natural to me. It doesn't feel resonant. If I meet my partner with understanding, it feels more like me. So when a thought appears, can I meet that thought with understanding? When I have learned to meet my thoughts with understanding, I meet you with understanding. What could you say about me that I haven't already thought? There *are* no new thoughts—they're all recycled. We're not meeting anything but thoughts. The external is the internal projected. Whether it's your thinking or my thinking, it's the same. Let's meet it with understanding. Only love heals.

It has been a life's work to make our partner wrong. Then when we enter inquiry, we lose. It's a tremendous shock. And it turns out to be grace. Winning is losing. Losing is winning. It all turns around.

When you own your share in something that your partner did to you, it's the sweetest thing in the world. You just feel humility, without the slightest urge to defend yourself. It leaves you completely vulnerable. This is the kind of vulnerability you want to lick off the pavement, it's so delicious.

My love is my business; it has nothing to do with you. You love me and that is not personal. You tell the story that I am this, or I am that, and you fall in love with your story. What do I have to do with it? I am here for your perception, as if I had a choice. I am your story, no more and no less. You have never met me. No one has ever met anyone.

It's not your job to love me—it's mine.

When you believe the thought "My husband should understand me," and the reality is that he doesn't, it's a recipe for unhappiness. You can do everything in the world to make him understand you, and he'll end by understanding what he understands. And if he understands you, what do you have? Just validation that your story is true. What he says he understands isn't even you, because as you manipulate his understanding, he can only understand the story you're telling. So even at its best, you're not being understood. We don't hear what you tell us; we hear what we think you're telling us. We impose our story on what you say, and that's what we understand. Are your thoughts what you punish him for?

I love telling a story that happened around 1997, when I was traveling every day, sharing The Work with people all over the world, day after day, constantly on planes, trains, and in cars. One night I got on a plane and I was really exhausted. It was a red-eye; that's what I could afford. I sat down next to a man, picked up his hand, put it in my lap, and fell asleep. I had no qualms about it, because I knew what he really was, and I knew that he loved me, though we had never met. He was still holding my hand when I woke up hours later. He was so sweet about it. He never asked my name. —But he wasn't any sweeter than the suitcase that fell from the overhead bin onto my head on another flight. It felt like a kiss as I collapsed. How do I know that I needed a hit on the head? Because that's what happened! No mistake. When you know that whatever you need is what you get, life becomes paradise. It's the perfect setup. Everything you need, and even more than you need, is always supplied, in abundance.

When I walk into a room, I know that everyone in it loves me. I just don't expect them to realize it yet.

The only possibility of being understood is to understand yourself. It's a full-time job. So if you inquire and come to see that what is is what you want, it's the end of any decisions about him. At that point you don't have to make any decision. There's no decision to torture him into understanding you. He continues to show you that his understanding is not your business.

OJAI VALLEY INN & SPA
COUNTRY CLUB ROAD, OJAI, CALIFORNIA 93023
805-646-5511

What is an example that will prove that you are not lovable? Rejection? If someone rejects you—and he could only do that because you don't match his beliefs about how he wants the world to be—it has nothing to do with you. Only an inflated ego could say that it had anything to do with you. Suppose your hand just moved for no reason, and he turns himself off with what he believes that means—do you have the audacity to think that you had something to do with it? You don't have that power, ever. If he yells at you, and you perceive that that is not love, *you* have hurt yourself, he hasn't. And if you are yelling within you that he shouldn't yell at

you, that is where the pain begins, not with
his yelling at you. You are arguing with reality,
and you lose.

When you say or do anything to please,
get, keep, influence, or control anyone or
anything, fear is the cause and pain is the
result. Manipulation is separation, and
separation is painful. Another person can
love you totally in that moment, and you'd
have no way of realizing it. If you act from
fear, there's no way you can receive love,
because you're trapped in a thought about

what you have to *do* for love. Every stressful thought separates you from people.

A dishonest yes is a no to yourself.

When a thought hurts, that's the signal that it isn't true.

Look at what you imagine is a flaw in your partner, and notice the ways that it gives you an opportunity to appreciate him or her. If you can't find these ways, you'll eventually have to strike out in anger—or you may just become frustrated at your lack of progress and attack yourself and her mentally. These attacks that you experience along the way are simply areas that need to be questioned, that's all. If the ways become obvious, you'll grow and grow into love without limit. And your partner will follow, and so will the rest of the world.

Reality unfolds perfectly. Whatever happens is good. I see people and things, and when it comes to me to move toward them or away from them, I move without argument, because I have no believable story about why I shouldn't; it's always perfect. A decision would give me less, always less. So "it" makes its own decision, and I follow. And what I love is that it's always kind. If I had to name the experience in a word, I would call it gratitude. Living, breathing gratitude. I am a receiver, and there's nothing I can do to stop grace from coming in.

Seeking love is how you lose the awareness of love. But you can only lose the awareness of it, not the state. That is not an option, because love is what we all are. That's immovable. When you investigate your stressful thinking and your mind becomes clear, love pours into your life, and there's nothing you can do about it. A friend sat in my room one morning—she's so courageous—with tears pouring down her face, saying, "I love you, Katie, I love you." The woman had no dignity. I saw her love for herself reflected through me. She saw that, too. And what I said to her was, "Isn't it fine to love at such a level and know you're not ever going to be disappointed in it?"

Sometimes you may appear to trade that love for the story appearing in the moment. It's like a little side-trip out into illusion. And when you investigate your story, you come back to where you always are.

When I don't look for approval outside me, I remain as approval. If I seek your approval, it's not comfortable inside me. And through inquiry I have come to see that I want you to approve of what you approve of, because I love you. What you approve of is what I want. That's love—it wouldn't change anything. It already has everything it wants. It already *is* everything it wants, just the way it wants it.

All the advice you ever gave your partner is for you to hear.

Your partner is your mirror. Except for the way you perceive him, he doesn't even exist for you. He is who you see he is, and ultimately it's just you again, thinking. It's just you, over and over and over and over, and in this way you remain blind to yourself and feel justified and lost. To think that your partner is anything but a mirror of you is painful. You don't see your partner; you just see what you believe about him. So when you see him as flawed in any way, you can be sure that that's where your own flaw is. The flaws have to be yours, because you're the one projecting them.

When you truly love yourself, it's not possible to project that other people don't love you. If your husband says he loves you, what does that have to do with you? He's just telling you who he is. He tells the story of how you're wonderful, how you're this and that, and he loves his story about you. He's projecting that you are his story. And then when you don't give him what he wants, he tells the story of how you're terrible, you're selfish—and what does *that* have to do with you? If my husband says, "I adore you," I think, "Good. I love that he thinks I'm his sweet dream." If he were ever to come to me and say, "The sorriest day of my life was when I married you," still, what would that have to do with me? He'd just be in a sad dream this time, and I might think, "Oh poor baby, he's having a nightmare. I hope he comes back soon." It's not personal. How can it have anything to do with me? I love him, and if what he says about me isn't true in my experience, I would ask him if there is anything that I can do for him. If I can do it, I will, and if it's not honest for me, I won't. He is left with his story.

You're living with God disguised as your husband, and he will show you all your unclear places, he will give you everything you need in order to get free. That's love.

When your partner is seen as God, your Work becomes very simple.

All love songs make sense if we remember what it is that we truly love. If the "you" of a song is another person, then the song is a lie. It has to be, because we can never find our completion in another person. It always comes back to us. So when we put God in the "you" of these songs, we see how true they all are. Every love song is written for God by God.

When you keep manipulating your partner to get her to love you, everything you do has that motive, even when you take her out to dinner. It's very painful. Awareness is a wonderful thing, and look forward to manipulating her again, because when we step into inquiry, our patterns change, and we become a total question mark. It's incredibly exciting that you don't even know who you are aside from your motives. And once you begin inquiring, you can take her out to dinner, and you are unlimited. Or you can not take her out to dinner, and you are unlimited. That's how it is. You love yourself totally, and she doesn't have to participate, so there is no motive in

"I love you." Isn't that fine? Without a motive, the pain disappears. Your thinking about what she was thinking about you was your hell. You had to puff yourself up to match all your beliefs about what you thought she was thinking. You had to be the Marlboro man. And when she has sex with you, you saw that as validation that your delusion was right.

If my husband were to say, "Stay home with me, I don't want you to be with people," and if I knew to be with people, I would say, "Thank you, sweetheart, I understand where you're coming from. And I'm going to be with people now." I've met him with some understanding. His is equal to mine. And I'm going to be with people now. I would tell him what I call the whole truth and nothing but the truth. "I need to be with people now" is just part of it. The rest of it is "I love you." "I love you, and I'm going to be with people now." But if I needed something from him, if I wanted his approval, that would be another story. So I turn it around—I want *my* approval. And if I sold out for approval, it wouldn't feel honest inside me; there would be no peace. I'd be treating my husband as not my nature if I were to seek his approval or love. It's unkind. And if I'm unkind to him, I'm unkind to me.

Once you open to love, you lose your whole world. It's over. Love leaves nothing. It's totally greedy. Our pain is in denying it. A boundary is an act of selfishness. There is nothing you wouldn't give to anyone if you weren't afraid. And you can't do that ahead of your time. You don't have to give anything for now, just investigate your thinking, do The Work. When you meet your thoughts with understanding, you discover that there's nothing to lose. So eventually there's no attempt at protection. Then giving everything you have becomes a privilege.

To exclude anything that appears in your universe is not love. Love joins with everything. It doesn't exclude the monster. It doesn't avoid the nightmare—it looks forward to it.

If I want love, I can't have it. I *am* love, and as long as I seek it from you, I can't know that. To love you is to separate. I *am* love, and that is as close as it can get.

Love says, "I love you no matter what." Love says, "You're fine the way you are." And that is the only thing that can heal; that is the only way you can join. If you think he's supposed to be different from what he is, you don't love him. In that moment you love who he is going to be when you're through manipulating him.

He is a throw-away until he matches your image of him.

You can't disappoint another human being. And another human being can't disappoint you. You believe the story of how your partner is not giving you what you want, and you disappoint yourself. If you want something from your partner and he says no, that's reality. It leaves you. And you can always give it to yourself.

You're just suffering from the belief that
there's something missing from your life.
In reality you always have what you need.

People think that relationships will make
them happy, but you can't get happiness from
the other person or from anywhere outside
you. A relationship is two belief systems
that come together to validate that there
is something outside you that can bring
you happiness. And when you think that
that's true, growing beyond your common
belief system means losing the other person,

because that's what you had together. So if you move forward, you leave this old belief system behind in what you call the other person, and then you feel it as separation and pain.

We are love, and there's nothing we can do about that. Love is our nature. It's what we are without our stories.

For the personality, love is nothing more than agreement. If I agree with you, you love me.

And the minute I don't agree with you, the minute I question one of your sacred beliefs, I become your enemy; you divorce me in your mind. Then you start looking for all the reasons why you're right, and you stay focused outside yourself. When you're focused outside and believe that your problem is caused by someone else, rather than by your attachment to the story you're believing in the moment, then you are your own victim, and the situation appears to be hopeless.

You can't love anyone; you only love your story about them.

There's a story I like to tell about Roxann, my daughter. She called me one day and said she wanted me to attend my grandson's birthday party. I told her that I had a commitment that day, I was going to do a public event in another city. She was so hurt and angry that she hung up on me. Then, maybe ten minutes later, she called me back and said, "I am so excited, Momma. I just did The Work on you, and I saw that there is nothing you can do to keep me from loving you." That is what we all have with the technology of this Work. There is nothing you can do to keep someone from loving you. And there is nothing anyone can ever do to keep you from loving them. It's not personal. It's about who you are.

Any time you find yourself wanting sympathy, you're trying to get someone to join you in your mythology. And it always hurts.

A relationship is two people who agree, two people who like each other's stories. We call it "love." And when our partner doesn't agree with our sacred story, the one we will stake our identity on, we divorce him. If someone says I'm unkind, I run to my husband and say, "Honey, so-and-so says I'm unkind." And he hugs me and strokes my cheek and says, "Well, that's just not true. Of course you're kind!" That way, I don't have to go inside and know the truth of the criticism for myself. I get my ally to fight on my side, and I call his agreement "love." If I go home and say, "Sweetheart, so-and-so says I'm unkind," and he says, "Well, you know, sometimes you *are* unkind, and here's how," and if I would rather have him agree with me than tell the truth, I'll feel hurt and angry, and then I'll go out and find a friend who *will* agree with me. Maybe that will work! But then sooner or later it becomes too painful. So I have to stop and go inside and set myself free. My husband can't give me that. Only I can give me that.

When you believe the thought that anyone should love you, that's where the pain begins. I often say, "If I had a prayer, it would be 'God spare me from the desire for love, approval, or appreciation. Amen.'" To seek people's love and approval assumes that you aren't whole.

The only relationship that is ever going to be meaningful is the relationship you have with yourself. When you love yourself, you love the person you're always with. But unless you love yourself, you won't be comfortable with someone else, because they're going to challenge your belief system, and until you inquire, you've got to do war to defend it. So much for relationship. People make these unspoken contracts with each other and promise each other that they won't ever mess with the other person's belief system, and of course, that's not possible.

How do you react when you think you need people's love? Do you become a slave for their approval? Do you live an inauthentic life because you can't bear the thought that they might disapprove of you? Do you try to figure out how they would like you to be, and then try to become that, like a chameleon? In fact, you never really get their love. You turn into someone you aren't, and then when they say

"I love you," you can't believe it, because they're loving a façade. They're loving someone who doesn't even exist, the person you're pretending to be. It's difficult to seek other people's love. It's deadly. In seeking it, you lose what is genuine. This is the prison we create for ourselves as we seek what we already have.

Romantic love is the story of how you need another person to complete you. It's an absolutely insane story. My experience is that

I need no one to complete me. As soon as I realize that, everyone completes me.

Hurt feelings or discomfort of any kind cannot be caused by another person. No one outside me can hurt me. That's not a possibility. It's only when I believe a story that I get hurt. And I'm the one who's hurting me by believing what I think. This is very good news, because it means that I don't have to get someone else to stop hurting me. I'm the one who can stop hurting me. It's within my power.

Everything is equal. There is no this person or that person. There's only One. And that's the last story. It doesn't matter how you attempt to be disconnected, it's not a possibility. The thought that you're believing is an attempt to break the connection. But it's only an attempt. It can't be done. That's why it feels so uncomfortable. It's an attempt to identify as an "I." And that's a full-time job, until it's not.

Only you can kick yourself out of paradise. So if you are Adam, and you look to Eve for completion, you have just kicked yourself out of paradise. You could just experience your own nature, which is to love yourself, and therefore her, with no separation. But if you want something from her, if you think you need her love or approval, you suffer. There's only one way I can use you to complete me and that is if I judge you, inquire, and turn it around.

The worst loss you've experienced is the greatest gift you can have.

Who would you be in people's presence without the story that anyone should care about you, ever? You would be love itself. When you believe this myth that people should care, you lose caring about people and yourself. Love can't come from out there; it can only come from inside you. The way that I know that is because it does. I was once walking in the desert with a man who began to have a stroke. We sat down, and he said, "Oh, my God, I'm dying, do something." I just sat there beside him, loving him, looking into his eyes, knowing that we were miles from a phone or car. He said, "You don't even care, do you?" I said, "No." He was talking through one side of his mouth because the other side had become paralyzed, and when I said "no," he started to laugh, and I did too. And then his faculties returned. The stroke came to pass, not to stay. The power of love. I wouldn't leave him for a caring.

You've never reacted to someone else. You project meaning onto nothing. There's nothing separate out there. And you react to the meaning you've projected. Loneliness comes from an honest place—you're the only one here. There are no humans here. You're it. This world doesn't even exist. When you investigate your thoughts and stop believing your projections, you come to realize that. It's the end of the world. The end of a world that never existed anyway.

I am always what I judge you to be in the moment. There's no exception. I am my own pain. I am my own happiness.

As long as you believe any concept, you're going to impose it onto your husband, your wife, your lover, your children. Sooner or later, when you don't get what you want from them, or when they threaten what you think you have, you're going to impose this concept onto them, until you meet it with some understanding. This is not a guess—this is what we do. We're not attached to people; we're attached to concepts.

Nothing can cost you someone you love. The only thing that can cost you your husband is if you believe a thought. That's how you move away from him. That's how the marriage ends. You are one with your husband until you believe the thought that he should look a certain way, he should give you something, he should be something other than what he is. That's how you divorce him. Right then and there you have lost your marriage.

Have you noticed how you get really happy when your partner does what you want? So you have to become a controller to put him in a position where he always does what you want.

I say, be grateful when he does what you want, and when he doesn't, skip the middleman and do it yourself.

Until you are loyal to yourself, you can't be loyal to another person.

Defense is the first act of war. If you tell me that I'm mean, rejecting, hard, unkind, unfair, I say, "Thank you, sweetheart, I can find all these in my life, I have been everything you say, and more. Tell me everything you see, and together we can help me understand. Through you, I come to know myself. Without you, how can I know the places in me that are unkind and invisible? You bring me to myself. So, sweetheart, look into my eyes and tell me again. I want you to give me everything." This is how friends meet. It's called integrity. I am all things. If you see me as unkind, that is an opportunity for me to go inside and look at what appears in my life. Have I ever been unkind? I can find it. Have I ever acted unfairly? That doesn't take me long to acknowledge. If I'm a bit cloudy about it, my children can fill me in. What could anyone call me that I couldn't find at some time in my life? If you say one single thing that I have the urge to defend, that thing is the very pearl waiting inside me to be discovered.

No one can leave you, only you can do that. Whatever his commitment is, your commitment is what you can count on, until it changes. A long-term commitment is for this very moment. Even if he says he is committed to you forever, you can never know that, because as long as you believe that there is a "you" and a "him," it is only a personality committing to a personality, and personalities don't love, they want something.

Until you can be happy that he's gone, for *his* sake (which is for your sake), your Work is not done. So it's good that your thoughts wake you up in the middle of the night curled up in a ball of terror. Do The Work on these projections that are so powerful. You are your own freedom. Look at how you've lived with him, what you have done to make sure that he thought you were "the one." You've lost your life, you think you have no life without him.

It's good that he leaves you, so that you can come to know who you really are.

I once spoke with a man who had been doing The Work for a while. His wife fell in love with another man, and instead of going into sadness and panic, he questioned his thinking. "'She should stay with me'—is it true? I can't know that. How do I react when I believe the thought? Extremely upset. Who would I be without the thought? I would love her and just want the best for her." This man really wanted to know the truth. When he questioned his thinking, he found something extremely precious. "Eventually," he said, "I was able to see it as something that should be happening, because it was. And I was able to say to my wife, 'Tell me everything about it, as if I were your best girlfriend.' She didn't have to censor any of it to protect me. It was amazing to hear about her experience. I felt so much joy for her. It was the most liberating experience I ever had." His wife moved in with the other man, and he was fine with that, because he didn't want her to stay if she didn't want to. A few months later, his wife hit a crisis point with her new lover and needed someone to talk to. She went to her best friend—her husband. They calmly discussed her options. He really loved her and just wanted her to be clear about what she wanted. She decided to get a place of her own where she could work things out, and eventually she went back to her husband. Through all this, whenever the man found himself mentally at war with what was happening, and experiencing pain or fear, he inquired into the thought he was believing at that moment, and returned to a calm and cheerful state of mind. He came to know for himself that the only possible problem he could have was only his own uninvestigated thinking. His wife gave him everything he needed for his own freedom.

A commitment is your truth, and there's no higher and no lower. You are committing yourself to your own truth. "I love, honor, and obey you, and I may change my mind." That's as good as it gets. I'm married only to God—reality. That's where my commitment is, for better or for worse. It can't be to a particular person. And my husband wouldn't want it any other way. So unless we marry the truth, there's no real marriage.

How would you function if you didn't have your pain and unhappiness? I am asking you to seriously go inside. How would it be if you smiled all the time, if you were free all the time? It would mean that you didn't have control and couldn't manipulate people, that insane idea wouldn't even occur to you. This is how you manipulate: "You should be with me," "If you leave I'll be miserable." You use these thoughts to get us to agree with your story that there is misery in this world, though the truth is that in your essence you are love, whether you like it or not. You can know that because one thought away from love, and you hurt.

We marry ourselves, or there is no marriage. That is the only love affair that's real. I am married within myself, I love myself, and that's what I project onto everyone. I am a lover of what is, and I don't want anything else. I only know I want to be here with you now. I *am* here with you, that's how I know that I want to be. It wasn't planned, it's simply unfolding. I love you completely, and you don't even have to participate, so there's no motive in "I love you." Isn't that fine! I can love you completely, and you have nothing to do with it. There is nothing you can do to keep me from the intimacy that I experience with you. When you have a stressful belief about your partner, you have separated from yourself, divorced yourself, and therefore you have divorced him, and it hurts. When you move away from yourself to your partner, you have divorced yourself. So when we have no beliefs about how reality should look, we're truly married, and it doesn't hurt. It's internal. There is no relationship outside that.

I can't feel your pain. That's not possible. If someone hits you and I believe that I "feel" it, I am projecting what that must feel like, and *that* is the pain I feel. I remember the time when someone hit me, and I feel my own story. In reality, there's no pain for me. There aren't two of us in pain; there's only one. Who would I be without my story? Pain-free, happy, and totally available if someone needs me. I hear people say that compassion means feeling someone else's pain, as if that were even possible. And how are you most present, most available—when you're in pain or when you're clear and happy? When someone is hurting, why would they want you to be hurting too? Wouldn't they rather have you totally present and available?

How can you be present for people if you believe that you're feeling their pain? If a car runs over someone and you're in terror, projecting what it must feel like, you're paralyzed. But sometimes in a crisis like that, the mind loses its reference, it can't project anymore, you don't think, you just act, you run over and pick up the car before you have time to feel or plan or think "This isn't possible." It happens in a split second. Who would you be without your story? The car is up in the air.

"If you loved someone with all your heart, you would be sexual"—can you absolutely know that that's true? What happens when you believe the thought that you can't get too close to a man or you'd be sexual? How does it feel when you think you have to hold yourself back from love? Who would you be without the story "I would be sexual if I fell into his arms"? You would be you, naturally. It's a very painful thing, the fear of oneself. Through the power of inquiry, you come to realize for yourself that you are love. There's nothing you can do about it.

A commitment is my truth in the moment. And if I want commitment, I'm going to find it only inside myself right now. If I want someone else to be committed to me, or if I want to be committed to someone else, it's hopeless, because it's personality committing to personality, and, as I often say, personalities don't love, they want something. When I commit to something, I follow it through, and I reserve the right to change my mind. Commitment is a wonderful path. It happens one moment at a time. I promise in one moment, and then in another moment I may change my mind. I keep my word until I don't. And people tell me that in their experience I do keep my commitments. If someone says that I didn't, I say, "Isn't that interesting! I changed my mind, or really, *it* changed. I'm not doing it, it's doing me. I can see that you really believe that I should have kept my commitment. It changed. And, if we wait, it could change back." And it could. I'm not doing it.

How do you know that you don't need a romantic partner? You don't have one. How do you know that you need one? Here he is! You don't call the shots on this. It's better that you don't. That way you can give yourself everything. What do you need a partner for? To fill your hunger? Is that true? All your adult life you've thought that you needed a partner, and you're still hungry. So how many partners does it take to fill you? I'm not saying that you don't need a partner. This is about your own truth. Just go in and experience it. Need yourself, whether or not you find a partner. In the meantime, you are waiting just for you.

Do you want to meet the love of your life?
Look in the mirror.

How do you treat your husband when you want him to love you? Can you see a stress-free reason to want him to love you, or to want anyone on this planet to love you? If I have the thought I want my husband to love me, it's not love. I want him to love whoever he loves. I may as well, because that's what he does anyway. I know I can't redirect it; I'm not a fool anymore. And people call that love, but I am just a lover of what is. I know the joy of loving, so I know it's not my business how he directs his love. My business is to love him.

Have you noticed how many times you try to control what comes in by giving rather than receiving? What happens when you just stand there and receive? The receiving *is* the giving. It's the most genuine thing you can give back. When someone comes to hug me, I don't have to hug them back. To receive it—you can die in that! To receive it is to die to pain, and to be born into love and laughter.

I was privileged to be married to someone who had zero interest in inquiry. And if I had believed that he needed The Work, *I* would have needed The Work. If I had believed that he needed to trust me, *I* would have needed to trust him. And I did trust him. I trusted him to do exactly what he did. So there was nowhere I could go but a perfect marriage. If I hadn't loved him with all my heart, I would have been insane. It had nothing to do with him. And that didn't mean I had to live with him.

The thing you're terrified of losing—you've already lost it. You may not have noticed that yet, and it may take you a while to grieve, and then you may realize that there was never anything to lose.

To believe the story that someone has left you is to leave yourself. That's how you divorce yourself. Every time you're in your partner's business, dictating whom he should be with, whom he should or shouldn't leave, you have left yourself, and the effect of that is loneliness and terror. Until you question what you believe, you remain the innocent cause of your own suffering.

The voice within is what I'm married to. All marriage is a metaphor for that marriage. My lover is the place that an honest yes or no comes from. That's my true partner. It's always there. And to tell you yes when my integrity says no is to divorce that partner.

No one who thinks "I should love myself" knows what love is. Love is what we are already. So to think that you should love yourself when you don't is pure delusion. Isn't the turnaround truer? "I shouldn't love myself." How do you know that you shouldn't love yourself? You don't! That's it, for now. The truth is no respecter of spiritual concepts. "I should love myself"—ugh, on what planet? Love is not a doing. There is nothing you have to do. And when you question your mind, you can see that the only thing that keeps you from being love is a stressful thought.

When you know who you are, there is no one you can't get along with. It takes only one, and that one is you. You can go downtown and pick a perfect stranger and get married and have a happy life. You are always with the perfect mate.

I don't want people's approval. I want people to think the way they think. That's love. Manipulating and trying to change someone is like trying to rape his mind. "You there! Stop your internal life and focus over here, on me! I absolutely know that it's in your best interest to approve of me. I want that, and I don't care what *you* want." But you can't control someone else's thinking. You can't even control your own.

There's no one thinking anyway. It's a house of mirrors. Seeking approval means being stuck in the thought "I'm a this," this little speck, this limited thing.

Marry yourself, and you have married us. We are you. That's the cosmic joke.

If my husband says, "Would you please bring me a cup of tea?" I know what my joy is—he just told me. That's how I know what to do. I know what it feels like when he brings me a cup of tea, the joy and gratitude that simple act gives me. The belief that he should get it for himself, or that he's using me, or that it's not my turn—that's what hurts. There is no belief that can stand up to inquiry, no genuine inquiry that can leave me as anything but love. Me serving me. To give him anything he wants is to give it to myself.

The reality is that without a story you are genderless, not male, not female, not even human. You're not anything. It is not anything, it's more than that. It's all-inclusive, it doesn't even question, there are no questions in the void, there is only the experience of it. And not even that.

We use our beauty, our cleverness, our charm, to capture someone for a partnership, as if he were an animal. And then when he wants to get out of the cage, we're furious. That doesn't sound very caring to me. It's not self-love. I want my husband to want what he wants. And I also notice that I don't have a choice. That's self-love. He does what he does, and I love that. That's what I want, because when I'm at war with reality, it hurts.

There's a lot to be said for monogamy. It's the ultimate symbol for One, because it keeps your mind focused on one primary person. You just have to undo everything about him, every story about him that rises up in your mind. Monogamy is a sacred thing, because the mind can be very still in that position. One person will give you the experience that a million people could give you. There's only one mind. Your partner will bring up every concept ever known to humanity, in every combination, so that you can come to know yourself. If you can just learn to love the one you're with, you have met self-love.

Without beliefs attached, sex is just like breathing or walking. It's beauty, it's you. But when you go into it seeking things like satisfaction, ecstasy, intimacy, connectedness, romance, don't count on finding them.

"An erection means that you're sexually aroused"—is that true? Are you sure? Do you believe everything you think? What does it really mean? It's an erection. That's it. The story you tell about it is where your suffering begins. For example, if you have the belief that you should put your erection somewhere, and there is nowhere to put it, that's what is hurting you. If you didn't believe the thought that you should do something with it, you would simply join with it, you'd become it, it would be a complete experience—the beginning, the middle, and the end. No climax, no ejaculation, just a beautiful erect penis, coming from nowhere, and with nowhere to go.

Your partner has nothing to do with your experience of making love—nothing. You touch him and you tell the story of what that means. He touches you, and you tell the story about what that means, and you turn yourself on, or you turn yourself off. If you believe the thought that he is touching you in the wrong way, you turn yourself off. You think you know something. The truth is that it's God making love with God, and there are no rules. And if you want to participate, be fully present. Your partner is not supposed to participate, he is just your story: "He's doing it right," "He's doing it wrong," "He's thinking this," "He's thinking that," "If he really loved me he would…" etc. On and on, and it's nothing but your story.

Without your story, have you ever really experienced sex? Never. No one ever has. We all have a story about what sex is. You are trying to get it to match your story about it: it's good, it's bad, you're a good lover, you're not, he should do this, he should do that. You're always trying to live up to your own story. What happens through sex is that you have beliefs about who he is, who you are, what your touch means, what his touch means, what this sensation means, what that emotion means. You tell yourself a story about all of it, and you call it good or bad. Who would you be without your story? You'd be free. To not know is my favorite part. And the truth is, you *don't* know. Without your story, you would have sex and love it, or not have sex and love it. It would just be what it is.

No one is mentally ill, no one is frigid: these are just terms we use to separate ourselves, to stay lost. You tell the story of who men are, and what sex is, and you freeze yourself up. You are not frigid, you're attached to an unquestioned story. Question your beliefs, and who knows what kind of lover you'll be? It has nothing to do with sexual pleasure. When you meet your thoughts with understanding, you meet yourself. You become your own lover. Ultimately that's whom you're sleeping with.

If my husband were to have an affair and that were not okay with me, I would still love him with all my heart. What I might say to him is this: "I see that you're having an affair, sweetheart, and I notice that when you do that, something inside me tends to move away from you. I don't know what that is, I only know that it's so, it mirrors your movement away from me, and I want you to know that."

And then if he were to continue his affair, to prefer to spend his time with another woman, I might notice that I was moving away or not, but I wouldn't have to leave him in anger. There is nothing I can do to stay with him, and there is nothing I can do to divorce him. I'm not running this show. I might stay with him, or I might divorce him in a state of total love, and think, "This is fascinating, I'm divorcing him now," and I would probably laugh and move on, because there is no war in me. And someone else would be divorcing him thinking, "He shouldn't have had the affair," "He hurt me," "He doesn't deserve me," "He broke his promises," "He's a heartless bastard." Either way, the motion is the same. The only difference is the story. You're going to make the trip either way: the question is, are you going to go kicking and screaming or are you going to go in dignity, generosity, and peace? You can't dictate this, you can't fake it, you can't make yourself be spiritual or loving. Just be honest and question your thinking and notice. Then when people say, "Oh, it's a terrible thing, this divorce," you might say, "I understand how you see it that way, and that's not my experience at all."

Love is so greedy for itself that it will leave you nothing. And when you're feeling that if you don't give it away you'll die in it, there's nothing you can do. All you can do is *be* it. You let it consume you. You sit in it and die. And when you are love, "something" is equal to "nothing." "I" is equal to "I."

Love wouldn't deny a breath. It wouldn't deny a grain of sand or a speck of dust. It is totally in love with itself, and it delights in acknowledging itself through its own presence, in every way, without limit. It embraces it all, everything from the murderer and the rapist to the saint to the dog and cat.

The difference between pleasure and joy? Ohhh…the distance is from here to the moon! From here to another galaxy! Pleasure is an attempt to fill yourself. Joy is what you are.

There is no way to join your partner except to get free of your belief that you want something from him, and then to give yourself to him totally. That's true joining. Our nature is to give, but we get confused about what it is that we're to give. The truth that you experience is how I join with you, that's how you touch me, and you touch me so intimately that it brings me to tears. I don't know what it is that you're doing, but I have joined you, and you don't have a choice. And I can do this over and over and over, endlessly, effortlessly. It's called making love.

When you come to the place where you don't want anything from your partner, it's like "Bingo! You just won the lottery!" If I want something from my partner, I need to take a look at my thinking. Because I already have everything. We all do. That's how I can sit here so comfortably: I don't want anything from you. I don't even want your freedom, if you don't. I don't even want your peace. But if *you* want it, that's all that's left of my want. So I'm going to join you there, because I remember what it was to want. And if you're not interested in your freedom, then that's what I want. I want your heaven, I want your hell, I want whatever you want, because I love you.

Love is so vast within itself. It's where you die. You don't die into fear; you die into love. It's so vast that it will burn you up. It's so jealous and greedy for itself mirrored back that it will leave you nothing. And when you're feeling that if you don't give it away you'll die in it, it's so vast that there's nothing you can do with it. All you can do is be it.